j595.76 Penny, Malcolm
P   Discovering beetles

$10•40

Discovering

BEETLES

Malcolm Penny

The Bookwright Press
New York · 1986

Discovering Nature

Discovering Ants
Discovering Bees and Wasps
Discovering Beetles
Discovering Birds of Prey
Discovering Butterflies and Moths
Discovering Flies
Discovering Frogs and Toads

Discovering Crickets and Grasshoppers
Discovering Rabbits and Hares
Discovering Snakes and Lizards
Discovering Spiders
Discovering Squirrels
Discovering Worms

Further titles are in preparation

All photographs from Oxford Scientific Films

First published in the
United States in 1986 by
The Bookwright Press
387 Park Avenue South
New York, NY 10016

First published in 1986 by
Wayland (Publishers) Limited
61 Western Road, Hove
East Sussex, BN3 1JD, England

© Copyright 1986 Wayland (Publishers) Limited

ISBN 0-531-18095-6
Library of Congress Catalog Card Number: 86-70991

Typeset by Alphabet Typesetters Limited
Printed in Italy by Sagdos S.p.A., Milan

Cover This colorful beetle is found in Trinidad. Its black and yellow markings may warn that it is poisonous.

Frontispiece *A rhinoceros beetle from the Solomon Islands.*

Contents

1
Introducing Beetles

Longicornis beetles on a leaf in Central America. Their black and yellow colors make them look like wasps.

Beetles Around the World

There are about 300,000 different kinds of beetles; they are the most successful group of animals in the world. The main reason for the success of beetles is that among them they can eat almost anything, animal or plant, living or dead. Some are serious pests, because their **larvae** eat stored food, farmers' crops, or lumber. A few others are helpful to humans, for example those that hunt crop-eating pests, or the dung beetles, which get rid of animal droppings by using them as food for themselves or their young.

The biggest beetles live in hot countries; the hercules beetle in Central America can be 19 cm (7 in) long. The goliath beetle in Africa is only 11 cm (4 in) long, but with its sturdy build and thick armor is the heaviest in the world, weighing as much as 100 g (3½ oz). The smallest are almost too tiny to see — smaller than the period that ends this sentence.

Most beetles are seldom seen because they live beneath stones, among dead leaves, or under the bark of trees. More often seen is the ladybird beetle (the ladybug). The ladybug is probably the best-loved insect of all. Most people like beetles, perhaps because many of them are brightly colored, like living jewels.

The hercules beetle is one of the biggest beetles in the world.

A Beetle's Body

An adult beetle, like all other insects, has three main parts to its body: the head, the **thorax**, and the **abdomen**. All three parts are protected by hard, often shiny armor. The middle section, the thorax, contains the muscles, which drive three pairs of legs and two pairs of wings, which are all attached to the thorax.

The front wings are what make a beetle look like a beetle. They are stiff and shiny, and are kept folded back over the abdomen, side by side, except when the beetle is flying. The rear wings, which are used for flying, are folded underneath the front wings, and protected by them when not in use.

The abdomen contains the beetle's digestive system, its **ovaries** or **testes**, and its breathing apparatus. Like most insects, a beetle breathes through airholes in the sides of its abdomen.

Above *This very colorful insect is a bark beetle.*

The head of a beetle carries its **antennae** and **palps**, which it uses for feeling and smelling, two eyes, which may be large or small, depending on the beetle's way of life, and its jaws. Some hunting beetles have long sharp jaws like pincers. Others, which eat leaves, have jaws more like a pair of scissors.

THE BODY OF A GREEN TIGER BEETLE

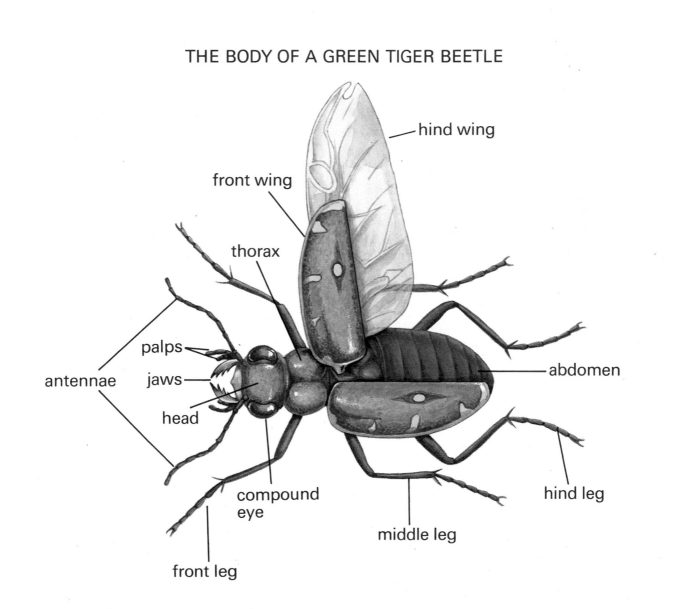

hind wing

front wing

thorax

palps

antennae

jaws

head

compound
eye

front leg

abdomen

hind leg

middle leg

2
Beetles Everywhere

A shining leaf chafer beetle takes off. Its front wings have been raised to expose its rear wings.

Flying Beetles

Almost all beetles can fly. There are a few sorts that cannot, because their front wings are joined together to make their armor stronger.

To take off, a beetle must first raise its front wings until they point slightly upward and forward, and then stretch out its rear wings. The rear wings are usually folded in thirds, but they can be opened very quickly with the jointed tubes that support them, like the ribs of an umbrella.

Most beetles like to climb to a high point, like the tip of a blade of grass, before they spread their wings. If you pick up a ladybug and let it walk on your hand, it will usually climb to the end of a finger before it flies away. This is because the wings of most beetles are so long when they are unfolded that they would hit the ground if the beetle tried to take off from a flat

surface. The long-legged tiger beetles do not have this problem, and they can take off from the ground in an instant.

The front wings do not usually flap at all, though stag beetles can move them a little. Usually, they act like the

A click beetle from Venezuela with its wings open, ready for flight.

wings of an airplane, holding the flying beetle steady, and helping to keep it in the air.

Beetles in the Garden

Beetles can be a nuisance in the garden, though some of them are helpful to the gardener because they keep down the number of pests. One of the most annoying beetles, to farmers as well as to gardeners, is the wireworm, which is the underground larva of a common click beetle. Wireworms usually eat grass roots, but

The wireworm is a common pest in gardens and farmland. It eats the roots of plants.

if a farmer plows up grassland to plant corn, they will eat that instead. Wireworms also eat potatoes, burrowing inside them and leaving holes where disease can get in.

Chafers are large, sturdy beetles that eat leaves. The rose chafer, as its name suggests, eats rose petals as well. It is a very handsome beetle, and it will only damage a few blooms; perhaps a few rose chafers in a garden are not as bad as they might seem. The larvae of chafers live underground, and eat plant roots.

Among the gardener's friends are ladybugs. Both as larvae and as adults, they eat **aphids**. Another friend is the glowworm. Its larvae eat slugs and snails. Some of the ground beetles do the same.

Other ground beetles are very common in gardens but, because they hunt at night, they are very rarely seen in action.

A female glowworm attracts a male by lighting up the underside of the end of her abdomen.

Beetles in the House

Probably the most common beetle in houses is the woodworm beetle. Its natural home is in dead trees, where the larvae burrow through the wood until they are ready to emerge as adults. Every house contains dead trees, in the form of woodwork and furniture, and a great many houses have woodworm in them somewhere.

The adult beetle emerges through a neat round hole about the size of a pinhead. A little fine dust comes out with the beetle: finding this dust near the hole is a sign that it is a new one, and that the beetles are active. There are chemicals that poison the larvae and prevent new infestation, but the damage done by woodworm beetles cannot be repaired.

Other beetles attack stored food, but they are more common in warehouses and grocery stores than in houses, because most food is inspected carefully before it is sold. Carpet beetles often fly into houses and lay their eggs in quiet corners. Their larvae eat all kinds of fibers, from carpets and curtains to clothes.

The common black beetle which often lives in houses does no damage, in spite of its reputation for being "dirty." In fact, being a hunter, it

Below *The damage to this furniture was done by the larvae of woodworm beetles.*

probably helps by eating other small household creatures such as baby woodlice and silverfish.

A carpet beetle larva will eat the fibers of carpets, curtains and clothes and can do a lot of damage.

Beetles in the Water

There are several types of beetles that can live underwater, among them the beautiful great water beetle. The adults are shiny green with gold stripes, and they are powerful swimmers. The larvae, too, are active swimmers, with large jaws. They can catch and eat tadpoles and small fish.

Whirligig beetles live on the surface, exploring it to find insects that have fallen in. They get their name from the way in which they spin around with

The great silver water beetle is so called because it is surrounded by air, which gives it a silver sheen.

their food while they are eating it. Whirligig beetles have interesting eyes, divided into two, one part to see above the surface and the other below.

The silver water beetle gets its name from the shining bubble of air that surrounds it while it is swimming. This bubble gives us a clue as to how water beetles breathe. They all carry an air supply with them, often trapped by hairs, which hold the water away from their body. The larva of the great water beetle has an air-tube at its tail end, where two holes draw in enough air for a short diving excursion. Adult water beetles usually store air under their front wings, or sometimes along the whole of the under surface of the body. Whirligig beetles dive beneath the surface when they are alarmed, trailing a bubble behind them.

Right *Several whirligig beetles on the surface of the water.*

Above *A female water beetle with a bubble of air, at the end of her abdomen.*

3
Beetle Ways of Life

A longhorn beetle on a flower. In its larval stage it lives and feeds inside birch trees.

Plant-eaters

Most beetles are **vegetarians**, and there is a beetle to eat almost every kind of plant.

There is a huge family of leaf beetles, each with its favorite food. Poplar beetles and willow beetles eat large holes in poplar and willow leaves, and another leaf beetle eats only mint plants, leaving nothing but the bare stems. A different kind of leaf-eating beetle, the cockchafer, can cause serious damage to woodlands by eating all the leaves off the trees.

Only a few beetles eat grass, because grass blades are tough, and they offer little shelter from the beetle's enemies. The larvae of some small beetles are called "leaf miners," because they burrow inside leaves, leaving hollow spaces like the tunnels in a mine.

Bark beetles attack trees, eating the

rich food supply just below the soft bark of young stems. When she is ready to breed, the female hollows out a chamber under the bark, and lays eggs in notches along the side. When the larvae hatch, they make feeding burrows leading off the main chamber. Each kind of beetle leaves a typical pattern under the bark, like a signature.

Longhorn beetles start life under the bark, but as the larvae grow they burrow deeper into the wood. There they eat the tree's own food supply, by breaking into the tubes in which the food passes up the trunk. The adults emerge to feed outside the tree, often on pollen.

The larvae of the cockchafer beetle are pests to farmers and gardeners because they eat plant roots. The adult beetles eat leaves and can seriously damage large areas of forest.

Active Hunters

Most hunting beetles have long legs, large eyes, and fierce jaws. The best example of a hunter is the tiger beetle, which is the fastest runner of all beetles. It can move at 3.2 kph (2 mph) for about 7.5 cm (3 in) when it attacks prey. That might not sound very fast, but if the beetle were the size of a

One of the fastest hunting beetles is the green tiger beetle. It has large eyes and sharp jaws.

racehorse, it would be able to cover 16 m (17½ yd) at 400 kph (248 mph) from a standing start!

Ground beetles, too, are fast runners. At night, they often climb trees to look for food, coming down in the morning to hide under stones. Most of them eat whatever they can catch, cutting up caterpillars or other small animals with their sharp jaws.

Rove beetles are different, in more ways than one. Their short front wings allow their bodies to be more flexible than those of other beetles, enabling them to wriggle rapidly through thick grass or between the air spaces in loose soil. They feed by crushing and sucking their **prey** rather than chopping it up, probably to avoid losing bits of it in the dark.

Beetles that hunt slow-moving prey do not need to run fast. Ladybugs amble around slowly on nettles or rose bushes, eating aphids, which have no

Adult ladybugs and their larvae eat the same food – aphids.

way of escaping. Some beetles, which eat snails, are also slow-moving, but they have long narrow heads, so they can reach the snail with their jaws as it retreats into its shell.

Scavengers

A scavenger is an animal that feeds on what other animals leave behind – the remains of their prey, their droppings, or their dead bodies. Many beetles are scavengers.

When a whirligig beetle has found a dead or dying insect on the surface of a pond, it begins to spin around with it. The ripples this causes bring other

A burying beetle, or sexton beetle, with a dead vole, which it will bury to be used as food for its larvae.

whirligig beetles to the food.

Burying beetles scavenge on land. The adults dig away the soil from underneath the dead body of a small animal until it is buried, often as much as 20 cm (8 in) deep. They eat some of it themselves, and use the rest to feed

their larvae when they hatch.

There are many other beetles that scavenge on dead bodies, both as adults and larvae, including some that specialize in eating skin, feathers, and fur. One such specialist is known as the museum beetle because it often invades collections of stuffed birds and animals.

Scavengers perform a very valuable service to all other animals by clearing

A scavenging ground beetle feeding on a bat skeleton in a cave in Venezuela, South America.

away the rubbish. One particular kind of rubbish, which would cause very serious health problems for all animals if it were not cleared away, is **dung**. The beetles that do the work are so important that they deserve a chapter to themselves.

Dung Beetles

An example of what the world might be like without dung beetles was seen in Australia, after European settlers took the first cattle there. Australian beetles had never seen cowpats: they are specialists in making use of kangaroo droppings. The pastures became fouled with masses of cattle dung, and the grass stopped growing.

The answer was to send in some dung beetles from Africa. They were used to cattle droppings and soon the problem was solved. The dung was neatly buried and sweet grass grew once more.

The beetles that were sent to Australia were members of the scarab family. Many scarabs roll dung into

A dung beetle from South Africa guards its ball of manure before burying it in an underground chamber where it lays its eggs.

balls, and bury it in an underground chamber, where they lay their eggs. When the larvae hatch, they have plenty of food.

The ancient Egyptians watched scarabs. When the dung ball was buried, the beetles died, but the next year they reappeared out of the ground. Because they thought that the beetles had found the secret of life after death, the Egyptians held them sacred. They carved beautiful scarabs, often out of precious stones, to show dead people the way to the next world.

Nowadays, although we do not regard dung beetles as sacred, we recognize how important they are to the whole of the natural world.

Dung beetles are found all over the world. This one, which lives in cow manure, is from Europe. Dung beetles are very important because they dispose of manure.

Enemies of Trees

Many plant-eating beetles feed on parts of trees, but two kinds of beetles in particular cause serious damage: the pine weevils, and one kind of bark beetle.

Pine weevils eat the tender growing

A row of dead elm trees – a reminder of the damage caused by Dutch elm disease.

shoots of **conifers**, such as pine and fir trees. They interfere with the tree's growth, so that it becomes worthless as timber, and sometimes they kill it altogether. Their larvae grow in old stumps or dead branches, or sometimes under the bark of young trees. In North America and elsewhere, pine weevils are the worst enemies of the foresters who grow the trees that are used to build houses. A different type of pine beetle attacks Scots pine trees in northern Britain.

One of the worst enemies of trees is a bark beetle that lives in elms. The beetle itself is harmless to the tree, but it carries a **fungus** that causes Dutch elm disease.

The adult beetle makes tunnels under the bark, and the grubs burrow into the wood. The beetles carry **spores** of the fungus on their bodies. The fungus causes swellings in the tubes that carry water and food up and down the tree, so the tree dies. Between 1967 and 1975, almost every elm tree in southern Britain died of Dutch elm disease carried by elm bark beetles.

Above *Elm bark beetle larvae burrow deep into the wood of a tree to feed.*

Below *The feeding tunnels left behind by elm bark beetle larvae. The adult beetles feed just under the bark of the tree.*

4
A Beetle's Life Cycle

A firebeetle glows to attract a mate. When in flight its abdomen has an orange glow.

Mating and Laying Eggs

Beetles that hunt on the ground may meet by chance during the breeding season, but others need ways of making sure that males and females get together. Some female beetles produce a scent that the males can smell from far away, while other kinds produce a scent whether they are male or female, so that groups of them can gather to **mate** in a suitable place.

There are other ways of attracting a mate. The death watch beetle "ticks" by tapping its head on wood, and the female glowworm glows so that passing males can see her light.

Most beetles lay their eggs near a supply of food for the larvae when they hatch. Leaf beetles glue groups of eggs to suitable leaves, and some weevils roll a leaf round the eggs. Ladybugs lay their eggs in clumps on plants where aphids are common, often on stinging nettles. Dung beetles dig burrows in which they leave a supply of dung for the larvae to eat. Some dung beetles lay only one egg, and the female stays to feed the single larva when it hatches.

The tiger beetle lays her eggs one at a time in any suitable patch of sandy soil. As we shall see, her larvae can look after themselves.

After mating (top) *the seven-spot ladybug lays her eggs on nettles* (bottom).

The oak weevil drills a hole in an acorn (top) *in which to lay her eggs* (bottom).

Different Types of Beetle Larvae

Beetle eggs hatch into one of several different types of larvae, depending on the way in which the larva is to find its food. The two active stages in a beetle's life, the larva and the adult, usually eat different kinds of food. The larvae of hunting beetles are usually

This beetle larva, from Tanzania in Africa, is well protected by its prickly hairs.

hunters themselves, with long legs and well-developed jaws for chasing and killing their prey. Ground beetles and ladybugs are good examples.

One exception is the tiger beetle larva, which hunts in a very special way. It crouches in a vertical burrow with its head uppermost, level with the ground, holding on to the sides with its legs. When an ant or a caterpillar walks past, the larva reaches out of the hole and grabs the prey with its jaws, dragging it into the burrow to eat. The whole capture takes a fraction of a second.

The stout larvae of dung beetles and chafers have legs, but they are slow-moving. They need only to crawl around in a dung-chamber or through the soil to find food.

Wood-boring larvae, like those of bark beetles or woodworm beetles, have very short legs or none at all, though they have powerful jaws to chew their way through their food. Weevil larvae are even less active. The small white grubs hatch inside the bean or wheat grain that will be their only food until they reach the next stage in their life.

Seven-spot ladybug larvae hatching from the eggs. Ladybug larvae eat small insects such as aphids.

Turning into an Adult

To turn into an adult, a beetle must go through a period when it can hardly move, while its wings and other adult organs develop. This stage is called the **pupa**.

Hunting beetle larvae burrow under the ground or hide beneath leaves or stones before they become pupae. Wood-boring larvae come near to the surface, or sometimes dig their way right out, and then go back inside, closing the entrance with sawdust so that they will be able to escape as adults. Water beetle larvae climb out of the water and make a burrow in the ground nearby. Dung beetles and tiger beetles are already safely underground.

All these hidden larvae turn into pupae which usually have little props to hold them away from the damp surface. These props prevent the larvae's getting moldy while they wait

1. *A water beetle larva leaves the water to begin the change into an adult.*

to emerge as adults.

A few beetles stay above ground as pupae. Ladybugs and some leaf beetles turn into tough pupae, with strong outer coats. They cannot move at all, and they are frequently cleverly **camouflaged**, often to look like bird-droppings.

Eventually the skin of the pupa splits, and a shiny new adult emerges. As the new skin hardens in the air, it develops the colors of the adult beetle.

2. A water beetle pupa in its burrow under the ground.

3. A newly-emerged adult water beetle stays in its burrow until its outer shell hardens.

4. Still in its underground burrow, the adult water beetle's outer shell darkens as it hardens.

5. Almost fully hardened, the water beetle is ready to leave its burrow for a life in the pond it left as a larva.

5
Beetles and Their Enemies

When attacked, the blister beetle can produce a chemical that will burn an animal's skin.

Physical and Chemical Defenses

The hard wing-cases of a beetle form its main defense against enemies. They may be covered with bristles or spines to make them look less appetizing to birds. Large beetles can defend themselves by biting, and some small beetles "play dead" if they are disturbed. They fold in their legs and antennae, and drop to the ground where they are very hard to find.

Another form of defense is to produce chemicals. These may be evil-smelling or foul-tasting, or actually harmful to an attacker. Water beetles produce a substance that makes a fish feel sick if it tries to eat one. The fish soon learns to leave these beetles alone.

Blister beetles produce an unpleasant chemical that burns the skin of animals, including humans. Bloody-nosed beetles dribble a red

substance, which also burns, and ladybugs taste bad to birds and spiders. Birds learn to avoid all these beetles after one taste.

The most dramatic chemical defenses are used by the bombardier beetles. They too produce a poisonous blistering chemical, with a puff of steam from the back end: the chemical

A bloody-nosed beetle on someone's hand. It is so called because it dribbles a red, burning liquid if disturbed.

is boiling hot. All these beetles with chemical defenses are brightly colored, usually with stripes or spots, so that their enemies can recognize them, and keep away.

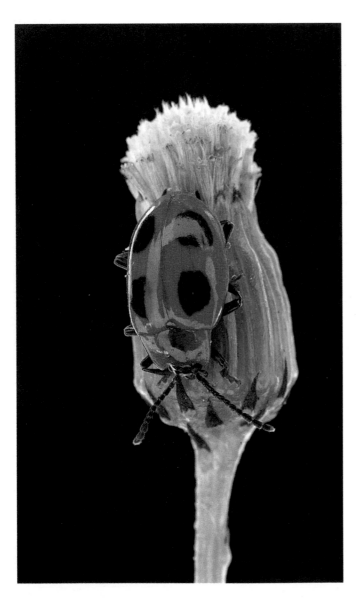

Escape

One way of escaping **predators** is to confuse them. Some beetles that are actually quite harmless are "mimics." They have patterns very similar to those of poisonous beetles. Birds are deceived by them, and by other disguises too. The wasp beetle pretends to be a wasp, and the devil's coach horse beetle raises its tail to look like a stinging insect.

Other beetles are camouflaged, usually by being drab colored to match soil or leaf litter, or green to match growing leaves. Some have blotchy patterns that make them hard to see, while others are very shiny so that they look less like food. Another way of escaping is to move very quickly. As you will find out when you try to catch

This beetle fools predators by mimicking the bad-tasting ladybird beetle (ladybug).

Left *The wasp beetle is harmless, but many predators avoid it for fear of being stung.*

Below *Click beetles sometimes escape enemies by quickly leaping into the air.*

one, ground beetles can run very fast, making for cover before their attacker can pounce.

Other beetles fly to safety, but the most surprising of all are the click beetles. Their first defense is to drop to the ground and "play dead." If they land right side up, they will soon run away, but if they land on their backs, they can leap suddenly into the air, as much as 35 cm (14 in) or more. They do this by means of powerful muscles, and a spring mechanism between thorax and abdomen.

Beetles as Pests

We have already met beetles that damage garden plants, injure trees, bore into furniture, chew carpets, and even attack stuffed animals. They can all be a serious nuisance, but the worst beetle pests of all are those that eat stored food. Most are specialists in one

Colorado beetles eat potato plants and can ruin a whole year's crop.

type of food. If they get into a large store of it, they will multiply and feed until the food is all gone.

Sometimes beetles make food inedible without eating it all. Stores of flour may be invaded by two different beetles, the khapra beetle, and the flour beetle. The khapra beetle produces a scent that drives flour beetles away, but the scent also makes the flour unfit for humans to eat. There is a beetle that eats bacon, one that bores holes into wine casks, and even one that eats tobacco.

There are two important pests of living crops, which have made life very difficult for humans. The Colorado beetle eats potato plants, destroying the whole crop in a bad year. Many countries take careful precautions to keep this pest out.

The other serious pest is the cotton boll weevil, which spread across the cotton-growing areas of the United

Khapra beetles and their larvae destroy stores of flour.

States in just thirty years, and now destroys over 200 million dollars' worth of cotton every year.

6
Learning More About Beetles

A black ground beetle. There are many different kinds of ground beetle, living in fields, woods and gardens.

Ladybugs, and black beetles in the house, are easy to see, but most beetles are not easy to find. After sunset an open window in a lighted room will bring in a few night fliers, such as small dung beetles and perhaps a cockchafer or a rose chafer.

If you put a cowpat that is dry on top into a bucket of water, and stir it gently with a stick, you will find a good sample of dung beetles. After their bath, they are surprisingly attractive, black and gold, or red, some of them scarabs and some rove beetles.

Ground beetles are best found by patiently watching, among leaf litter in woodland, or in a sunny but not too grassy field. If you sink a jelly jar into the ground until its rim is level with the surface, passing beetles will fall in, and you can study them.

If you catch any beetle to take a better look at it, be sure to return it to the place where you found it.

Beetles are easy to keep at home, provided you can supply the right kind of food. The next most important thing is to keep them covered – remember that almost all beetles can fly. An old net curtain will do as a cover, provided its pattern does not include any large holes.

Ladybugs will settle happily into a **vivarium,** living on fresh nettles or other plants, complete with aphids for them to eat. If you can find plants with ladybug larvae on them so much the better. You can watch them growing up and pupating, to emerge later as bright yellow adults. Their red and black spotted colors develop a few hours after the adult has emerged.

A newly-emerged seven-spot ladybird beetle is yellow. Gradually it darkens to red and its spots develop.

Glossary

Abdomen The rear part of an insect's body, containing the stomach and the ovaries or testes.

Antennae The two feelers on the head of an insect; antennae are sensitive to touch and smell.

Aphids Small, soft-bodied, plant-sucking insects. Green aphids are often called greenflies.

Camouflaged Hidden by colorings and markings that blend in with the surroundings.

Conifers Trees that produce cones, such as pines.

Dung Animal droppings, or manure.

Fungus (plural fungi) A plant without green coloration, for example mushrooms and molds.

Larva (plural larvae) The correct name for a grub, the form of an insect that emerges from the egg.

Mate To join as a pair; male and female animals mate so that the female's eggs can be fertilized by the male's sperm.

Ovaries The glands that make eggs, in the abdomen of female animals, the female's sex cells.

Palps The "feelers" around an insect's mouth, used for handling as well as tasting food.

Predators Animals that hunt and kill other animals for food.

Prey An animal that is caught by another animal for food.

Pupa (plural pupae, verb to pupate) The stage in the growth of an insect when the larva is broken down and reformed into the adult.

Spores The "seeds" of fungus, usually spread by wind, or carried by animals.

Testes The glands in the abdomen of male animals. The testes make sperm, the male's sex cells.

Thorax The middle part of an insect's body, between the head and the abdomen. The thorax bears the legs and wings.

Vegetarians Animals that eat only plants.

Vivarium A place where live animals are kept under natural conditions for study.

Finding Out More

If you would like to find out more about beetles, you could read the following books:

Fischer-Nagel, Andreas and Heiderose. *Life of the Ladybug.* Minneapolis, MN: Carolrhoda Books, 1985.

Johnson, Sylvia. *Beetles.* Minneapolis, MN: Lerner Publications, 1982.

----------. *Ladybugs.* Minneapolis, MN: Lerner Publications, 1983.

Milne, Lorus and Margery. *Nature's Clean-up Crew: The Burying Beetles.* New York: Dodd, Mead, 1982.

Patent, Dorothy and Paul Schroeder. *Beetles and How They Live.* New York: Holiday House, 1978.

Pope, Joyce. *Insects.* New York: Franklin Watts, 1984.

Simon, Hilda. *Our Six-Legged Friends and Allies: Ecology in Your Back Yard.* New York: Vanguard Press, 1972.

Index

Picture Acknowledgments

All photographs from Oxford Scientific Films by the following photographers: A.C. Allnutt 20; G.I. Bernard 12, 14, 18, 19 (top), 25, 28, 30, 35, 38, 40, 41; R. Blythe 15, 21; W. Cheng *frontispiece*; J.A.L. Cooke 9, 24, 29, 39 (left); D. Curl 26; S. Dalton 15, 19 (bottom), 34, 39 (right); E.R. Degginger (Animals Animals) 10; R.A. Mender (Mantis Wildlife) 36; J. Paling 17; A. Ramage 16, 23, 27, 31 (left), 33, 37, 42, 43; P.K. Sharpe 8, 22; P. & W. Ward 32; D. Wright 31 (right). Artwork by Wendy Meadway.